G000130902

by Iain Gray

Lang**Syne**

PUBLISHING

WRITING *to* REMEMBER

79 Main Street, Newtongrange,
Midlothian EH22 4NA
Tel: 0131 344 0414   Fax: 0845 075 6085
E-mail: info@lang-syne.co.uk
www.langsyneshop.co.uk

Design by Dorothy Meikle
Printed by Ricoh Print Scotland
© Lang Syne Publishers Ltd 2015

ISBN 978-1-85217-220-6

Boyd

MOTTO:
I trust.

CREST:
A right hand raised in benediction.

TERRITORY:
Ayrshire.

*Echoes of a far distant past
can still be found in most names*

Chapter one:

Origins of Scottish surnames

by George Forbes

It all began with the Normans.

For it was they who introduced surnames into common usage more than a thousand years ago, initially based on the title of their estates, local villages and chateaux in France to distinguish and identify these landholdings, usually acquired at the point of a bloodstained sword.

Such grand descriptions also helped enhance the prestige of these arrogant warlords and generally glorify their lofty positions high above the humble serfs slaving away below in the pecking order who only had single names, often with Biblical connotations as in Pierre and Jacques.

The only descriptive distinctions among this peasantry concerned their occupations, like Pierre the swineherd or Jacques the ferryman.

The Normans themselves were originally Vikings (or Northmen) who raided, colonised and eventually settled down around the French coastline.

They had sailed up the Seine in their long-boats in 900AD under their ferocious leader Rollo and ruled the roost in north east France before sailing over to conquer England, bringing their relatively new tradition of having surnames with them.

It took another hundred years for the Normans to percolate northwards and surnames did not begin to appear in Scotland until the thirteenth century.

These adventurous knights brought an aura of chivalry with them and it was said no damsel of any distinction would marry a man unless he had at least two names.

The family names included that of Scotland's great hero Robert De Brus and his compatriots were warriors from families like the De Morevils, De Umphravils, De Berkelais, De Quincis, De Viponts and De Vaux.

As the knights settled the boundaries of

their vast estates, they took territorial names, as in Hamilton, Moray, Crawford, Cunningham, Dunbar, Ross, Wemyss, Dundas, Galloway, Renfrew, Greenhill, Hazelwood, Sandylands and Church-hill.

Other names, though not with any obvious geographical or topographical features, nevertheless derived from ancient parishes like Douglas, Forbes, Dalyell and Guthrie.

Other surnames were coined in connection with occupations, castles or legendary deeds. Stuart originated in the word steward, a prestigious post which was an integral part of any large medieval household. The same applied to Cooks, Chamberlains, Constables and Porters.

Borders towns and forts – needed in areas like the Debateable Lands which were constantly fought over by feuding local families – had their own distinctive names; and it was often from them that the resident groups took their communal titles, as in the Grahams of Annandale, the Elliots and Armstrongs of the East Marches, the Scotts and Kerrs of Teviotdale and Eskdale.

Even physical attributes crept into surnames, as in Small, Little and More (the latter being 'beg' in Gaelic), Long or Lang, Stark, Stout, Strong or Strang and even Jolly.

Mieklejohns would have had the strength of several men, while Littlejohn was named after the legendary sidekick of Robin Hood.

Colours got into the act with Black, White, Grey, Brown and Green (Red developed into Reid, Ruddy or Ruddiman). Blue was rare and nobody ever wanted to be associated with yellow.

Pompous worthies took the name Wiseman, Goodman and Goodall.

Words intimating the sons of leading figures were soon affiliated into the language as in Johnson, Adamson, Richardson and Thomson, while the Norman equivalent of Fitz (from the French-Latin 'filius' meaning 'son') cropped up in Fitzmaurice and Fitzgerald.

The prefix 'Mac' was 'son of' in Gaelic and clans often originated with occupations – as in MacNab being sons of the Abbot, MacPherson and MacVicar being sons of the minister and MacIntosh being sons of the chief.

The church's influence could be found in the names Kirk, Clerk, Clarke, Bishop, Friar and Monk. Proctor came from a church official, Singer and Sangster from choristers, Gilchrist and Gillies from Christ's servant, Mitchell, Gilmory and Gilmour from servants of St Michael and Mary, Malcolm from a servant of Columba and Gillespie from a bishop's servant.

The rudimentary medical profession was represented by Barber (a trade which also once included dentistry and surgery) as well as Leech or Leitch.

Businessmen produced Merchants, Mercers, Monypennies, Chapmans, Sellers and Scales, while down at the old village watermill the names that cropped up included Miller, Walker and Fuller.

Other self explanatory trades included Coopers, Brands, Barkers, Tanners, Skinners, Brewsters and Brewers, Tailors, Saddlers, Wrights, Cartwrights, Smiths, Harpers, Joiners, Sawyers, Masons and Plumbers.

Even the scenery was utilised as in Craig, Moor, Hill, Glen, Wood and Forrest.

Rank, whether high or low, took its place with Laird, Barron, Knight, Tennant, Farmer, Husband, Granger, Grieve, Shepherd, Shearer and Fletcher.

The hunt and the chase supplied Hunter, Falconer, Fowler, Fox, Forrester, Archer and Spearman.

The renowned medieval historian Froissart, who eulogised about the romantic deeds of chivalry (and who condemned Scotland as being a poverty stricken wasteland), once sniffily dismissed the peasantry of his native France as the jacquerie (or the jacques-without-names) but it was these same humble folk who ended up over-throwing the arrogant aristocracy.

In the olden days, only the blueblooded knights of antiquity were entitled to full, proper names, both Christian and surnames, but with the passing of time and a more egalitarian, less feudal atmosphere, more respectful and worthy titles spread throughout the populace as a whole.

Echoes of a far distant past can still be found in most names and they can be borne with pride in commemoration of past generations who fought and toiled in some capacity or other to make our nation what it now is, for good or ill.

Chapter two:

In freedom's defence

By the time they were raised to the peerage by James II in 1454, the Boyds had already played a significant role in Scotland's history, not least through their selfless contribution to the cause of the Nation's freedom in the bitter and bloody Wars of Independence with England.

Some sources assert the name stems from the Gaelic 'buidhe', meaning fair.

One tradition is that the original ancestor of today's Boyds was Simon FitzAlan, known as Simon the Fair, who was either a nephew or a younger brother of Walter FitzAlan, the High Steward of Scotland who is recognised as the progenitor, or founder, of what became the Royal House of Stewart (or Stuart).

This explains why the Boyds, although a proud clan in their own right, are considered a sept, or branch, of the Stewarts, and why many today adopt the Royal Stewart tartan, although there is a Boyd sett.

Another explanation for the origin of the name Boyd is that it is a 'location' name, from the Gaelic 'Boid', referring to the island of Bute in the Clyde estuary.

Ayrshire became the homeland of the Boyds, with a Dominus Robertus de Boyd recorded as having witnessed a contract concerning the west coast town of Irvine in 1205.

This family of Boyds are thought to have been vassals of the powerful Anglo-Norman family of de Morville, but by the early thirteenth century they had risen to such prominence that they held their own lands in Ayrshire, particularly in the vicinity of Kilmarnock.

The Boyds appear to have been no sooner settled in Ayrshire than they found themselves embroiled in the cause of the nation's freedom.

They rallied to its defence at the battle of Largs, when Sir Robert Boyd was among a group of Ayrshire lairds raised by Alexander FitzAlan, in his role as High Steward, to repel a Viking invasion that threatened after the king of Scots, Alexander III, laid claim to the Hebrides.

Warned that Alexander was prepared to wrest the islands from Norwegian control by force if necessary, King Hakon of Norway embarked with a mighty fleet from Bergen in July of 1263.

His fierce band of sea raiders plundered and ravaged Kintyre, Bute, and Islay, before appearing off the west coast mainland township of Largs.

A storm blew many of the vessels onto the shore beneath the overhanging Cunningham hills on the night of September 30, and it was on top of these hills that FitzAlan hastily assembled a force of militia that included Sir Robert Boyd and his kinsfolk.

A party of militia emerged from their high eminence the following morning and engaged in a skirmish with a band of Norsemen attempting to salvage precious cargo from their stricken vessels.

The Scots drove them back to their

ships and returned that evening to gleefully loot the cargo.

Stung by the insult, King Hakon ordered a further attempt to retrieve the cargo the following day, October 1, resulting in what has become known as the battle of Largs but which in reality consisted of a series of disorganised skirmishes.

The Norsemen were driven back to their vessels, however, and King Hakon died a few weeks later in Kirkwall, Orkney: the threat to Scotland's western seaboard in general and invasion of the mainland in particular had been averted.

The victory is commemorated annually at Largs with the ceremonial burning of a Viking longboat.

Intriguingly, while 'I trust' is the motto of the Boyds, and a right hand raised in benediction is the crest, several of the family's coats of arms feature the word 'Goldberry'.

This is thought to be in commemoration of Sir Robert Boyd who, with only a small band of men, fought and defeated a force of the invaders several miles south of the site of the main battle of Largs, at a location known as Goldberry, or Goldberry Hill.

More than forty years later, the Boyds found themselves at the forefront the Wars of Independence after William Wallace raised the banner of revolt against the English occupation of Scotland in May of 1297.

An expert in the tactics of guerrilla warfare, Wallace and his hardened band of freedom fighters inflicted stunning defeats on the English garrisons, culminating in the liberation of practically all of Scotland following the battle of Stirling Bridge, on September 11, 1297.

Defeated at the battle of Falkirk on July 22, 1298, after earlier being appointed Guardian of Scotland, Sir William Wallace was eventually betrayed and captured in August of 1305, and, on August 23 of that year, he was brutally executed in London on the orders of a vengeful Edward I of England.

The bitter struggle continued under the leadership of the warrior king Robert the Bruce, however, and, in 1306, Duncan Boyd was killed by the English for swearing allegiance to him.

The struggle culminated in the battle of Bannockburn of June, 1314, when a 20,000-strong English army under Edward 11 was defeated by a Scots army less than half this strength.

Ironically, it was through a misguided sense of chivalry that the battle occurred in the first place.

By midsummer of 1313 the mighty fortress of Stirling Castle was occupied by an English garrison under the command of Sir Philip Mowbray.

Bruce's hotheaded brother, Edward, rashly agreed to a pledge by Mowbray that if the castle was not relieved by battle by midsummer of the following year, then he would surrender.

This made battle inevitable, and by June 23 of 1314 the two armies faced one another at Bannockburn, in sight of the castle.

It was on this day that Bruce slew the English knight Sir Henry de Bohun in single combat, but the battle proper was not fought until the following day, shortly after the rise of the midsummer sun.

The English cavalry launched a desperate but futile charge on the densely packed ranks of Scottish spearmen known as schiltrons, and by the time the sun had sank slowly in the west the English army had been totally routed, with Edward himself only narrowly managing to make his escape from the carnage of the battlefield.

Scotland's independence had been secured, to the glory of Bruce and his loyal army and at terrible cost to the English.

Sir Robert Boyd had been among Bruce's most able commanders at Bannockburn, and was rewarded with lands in Ayrshire that Bruce confiscated from his rivals, the Balliols, with Dean Castle, in Kilmarnock, becoming the main family seat.

Other branches of the family also flourished in Ayrshire, as the Boyds of Merton, Penkiln, Pitcon, and Trochrig.

Now a popular tourist attraction, Dean

Castle and its surrounding estate are now in the care of the East Ayrshire local authority.

As the power and influence of the Boyds increased following their elevation to the peerage in 1454, so to did their ambitions – and this was to prove fatal to their fortunes.

Chapter three:

Kidnapping and execution

Following the death of James II in July of 1460, Lord Boyd of Kilmarnock was appointed one of the regents of the young James III.

By 1466, his brother, Sir Alexander Boyd, held the powerful posts of Chamberlain of the Royal Household and governor of Edinburgh Castle, while his son, Thomas, held the influential post of the king's instructor in the military arts.

Consolidating their power, the Boyds actually kidnapped the king, persuading him to ratify an Act of Parliament that made them the sole guardians of the kingdom.

Their grip on the realm was further strengthened when Thomas Boyd married the king's sister, the Princess Mary, and assumed the titles of Earl of Arran and Kilmarnock.

But pressure from a powerful group of

rival nobles eventually led in November of 1469 to the Boyds being summoned before the king and Parliament to answer charges of treason.

Sir Alexander was executed, while Lord Boyd escaped to England and the Earl of Arran fled into exile in the Low Countries, where he died.

The Earl of Arran's marriage to the Princess Mary had been annulled, and all the Boyd estates and honours were forfeited – but they were restored again during the reign from 1542 to 1567 of Mary, Queen of Scots.

A later Lord Boyd was a staunch support-er of the ill-starred queen, fighting for her cause at the decisive battle of Langside on May 13, 1568.

The queen had escaped from Lochleven Castle, in which she had been imprisoned after being forced to sign her abdication by a body known as the Confederate Lords.

Lord Boyd was among a group of nobles, bishops, lairds, and others who signed a bond declaring their support for her, and they and their forces met an army raised by the Confederate

Lords at Langside, on the southern outskirts of Glasgow.

Mary's forces, under the command of the Earl of Argyll, had been en route to the mighty bastion of Dumbarton Castle, atop its near inaccessible eminence on Dumbarton Rock, on the Clyde, when it was intercepted by a numerically inferior but tactically superior force led by her half-brother, the Earl of Moray.

Cannon fire had been exchanged between both sides before a force of Argyll's infantry tried to force a passage through to the village of Langside, but they were fired on by a disciplined body of musketeers and forced to retreat as Moray launched a cavalry charge on their confused ranks.

The battle proved disastrous for Mary and signalled the death knell of her cause, with more than 100 of her supporters killed or captured and Mary forced to flee into what she then naively thought would be the protection of England's Queen Elizabeth.

Lord Boyd later showed his devotion to

his queen by visiting her periodically during the long exile she spent in England before her eventual execution in the Great Hall of Fotheringhay Castle, in Northamptonshire, in February of 1587.

Although the third Earl of Kilmarnock took the side of the Hanoverian government in the abortive Jacobite Rising of 1715, William, the fourth earl, proved loyal to the Jacobite cause in the 1745 Rising, eventually paying the ultimate price for his adherence to the cause.

Prince Charles Edward Stuart had arrived on the small Outer Hebridean island of Eriskay on July 22, 1745, landing on the mainland at Loch nan Uamh three days later.

The Stuart Standard was raised on August 19, at Glenfinnan, on Loch Shiel, and victory was achieved at the battle of Prestonpans, on the outskirts of Edinburgh, in September.

The confident prince and his army set off on the long march south to London a month later, to claim what was believed to be the rightful Stuart inheritance of the throne.

The army reached only as far as Derby,

Raising the Standard at Glenfinnan

however, before the controversial decision was taken in early December to withdraw back over the border.

Jacobite hopes were later dashed forever - at the battle of Culloden, fought on Drummossie Moor, near Inverness, on April 16, 1746.

In what was the last major battle fought on British soil, hundreds of clansmen died on the battlefield while hundreds of others died later from their wounds and the inhumane treatment of their government captors.

Although two of his sons were serving in the government ranks, the 40-year-old earl had joined the prince in Edinburgh and raised a troop of cavalry known as Kilmarnock's Horse.

They had advanced with the Jacobite army as far as Derby and were present at the battle of Falkirk on January 17, 1746.

Wounded and taken prisoner at Culloden, the abject Lord Boyd was being led bareheaded along the lines of the victorious Hanoverian army when his eldest son, who was serving as an ensign in the government forces, spotted the plight of his father and rushed forward to give him his own hat.

Imprisoned in the Tower of London, Lord Boyd was brought to trial for treason on July 28, 1746.

The statesman Horace Walpole, who was present throughout the trial, left a portrait for posterity of Lord Boyd, describing him as 'tall and slender, with an extreme fine person; his behaviour a most just mixture between dignity and submission.

'If in anything to be reprehended, a little affected, and his hair too exactly dressed for a man in his station; but when I say this it is not to find fault with him, but to show how little fault there is to be found.'

Pleading guilty, he threw himself on the mercy of the court, stressing that he had opted to surrender, rather than attempt to escape from the battlefield, but this proved to be of no avail: his head fell under the executioner's axe on Tower Hill on August 18, 1746.

The Boyd titles were forfeited, but Lord

Boyd's eldest son, through his mother, succeeded to the earldom of Erroll in 1758, and took the surname of Hay.

It was not until 1941 that a brother of the 22nd Earl of Erroll again assumed the proud name of Boyd and the title of Lord Kilmarnock.

Chapter four:

Exploration and the arts

Significant numbers of Ayrshire Boyds are known to have settled in Ireland during what was known as the Plantation of Ulster, from 1609 to 1613, and many later emigrated from there to North America, while others emigrated from Scotland itself to find a new life there.

Louise Arner Boyd, born in San Rafael, California, in 1887, was a renowned Arctic explorer and the first woman to fly over the North Pole – a feat she achieved at the age of 68.

Born into a wealthy family, Boyd funded and led her own expedition in 1928 in an abortive attempt to find the Norwegian explorer Roald Amunsden, who himself had vanished without trace during his own attempt to find the Italian explorer Umberto Nobile.

Despite her failure to find Amunsden, the

Norwegian government awarded her the Chevalier Cross of the Order of St Olav.

In the years 1931, 1933, 1937, she led scientific expeditions to both the east and north-eastern coasts of Greenland, and an area near the De Geer Glacier is now named Louise Boyd Land.

The intrepid explorer, who died in 1972, was also employed as a technical expert by the U.S. War Department during the Second World War.

In the world of science, Sir John Boyd Orr, the 1st Baron Boyd-Orr, born in the Village of Kilmaurs, near Kilmarnock, in 1880, was the doctor and biologist who in 1949 won a Nobel Peace Prize for his groundbreaking research into nutrition and his work with the United Nations Food and Agricultural Organisation.

The idealistic Boyd-Orr donated his Nobel Prize money to the cause of the creation of a united world government and universal peace.

William Merric Boyd, born in Australia in 1888 was the founder of a veritable artistic dynasty. An artist, sculptor, and ceramicist, Boyd, who died in 1959, is recognised as the father of Australian studio pottery.

He was the father of the artists Arthur Boyd and David Boyd, and the sculptor Guy Boyd, while he was the brother of the painter Helen Read, the writer Martin Boyd, and the landscape artist Penleigh Boyd.

A prominent figure in contemporary literature is the novelist and screenwriter of Scottish descent William Boyd, who was born in Ghana in 1952.

Educated at Gordonstoun School in Scotland and the universities of Nice, Glasgow, and Oxford, he published his first novel, *A Good Man in Africa*, in 1981, while working as a lecturer in English at Oxford University.

Other novels include *Brazzaville Beach*, and *An Ice Cream War*, while Boyd was made a Companion of the British Empire (C.B.E.) in 2005.

On the stage, William Boyd was the actor born in Cambridge, Ohio, in 1895 and who began his career in silent film romances but later achieved fame as the cowboy hero Hopalong Cassidy.

In contemporary times, Billy Boyd, born in Glasgow in 1968, is the actor best known for his role as the hobbit Peregrine Took in the *Lord of the Rings Trilogy* (2001-2003). He also played the role of Barrett Bowden in the 2003 film *Master and Commander: The Far Side of the World*.

A talented guitarist, drummer, and singer, Boyd is a graduate in dramatic arts from the Royal Scottish Academy of Music and Drama, and is also an accomplished stage actor.